KALI
YUGA

Cape Goliard Press

KALI YUGA

Robert Kelly

KALI YUGA

These small poems for the most part were composed between
1964 & 1968. "A Journey," "The Moon," and "The Islands"
are earlier, and were printed in *Origin*, second series, number
5, edited by Cid Corman. Others have appeared in *The Nation;*
Caterpillar; Helicon; Hardware Poets Occasional; Wild Dog;
Fubbalo; Matter; Set; some Buffalo NY newspaper; Allen de
Loach's anthology; *The Floating World; Guerilla;* Gerald
Stevenson's *Iowa Defender;* The last poem is reprinted from
a privately printed book, *Crooked Bridge Love Society.*

Designed printed and Published by Cape Goliard
Press Ltd., 10a, Fairhazel Gardens, London N.W.6.
50 Copies of this first edition have been signed
and numbered by the Author.
Printed in Great Britain.

U.K. SBN. P.206 61877-8 C.206 61876-X

this book: ta'wil for Helen

Kali Yuga

fourth age
age of Kali
age of black

when the woman
swings the arms of her soul
opens the light inside her

when the work is Destruction

putrefaction

get it all together
& go from there

out into open

RK, January 69

A JOURNEY

when the night carries me
to its own house I can
see someone getting out of
bed who looks at me &
has a white face, a woman
with full breasts & dark hair
who looks at me with her fingers

I have come to the cabin called
where the moon walks

THE MOON

by early morning
is down the western
sky. It is white and
blue covers it

in cloud. Wherever
you look there is
something setting, some
tired back outstretched

resting from work you
never dreamed of. It
is further away
than any other time.

You reach out and
get nothing. Who are
you to judge these men.
They live here too

afraid to turn the
light off, just trying
to draw one late blue
breath. You still have

nothing, the moon has
set, the sun rises, leave
them alone, there is
nowhere else.

THE ISLANDS

who knows those cities

forty miles
the name of a mountain

a clear day &
from our viewpoint
unsteady on harbor waves

unknown familiar shapes

having no reason no
reason for love

MUDRAS

1   The bones of her hands who is priestess of this altar
                naked at the dancing place
how can we bring her down into our time?

                                Where did that
we come from. West.

               Moving in relation
or lation, motion, outward. Herward. Her hard hands.

2   The old book talks about the form,
double-pointed ellipse, the shape of women,

                    finger touching finger
                    hand's heels joined,

a dark to look in, funnelling the dark of the hand's flesh
to a chink of lozenged light,

                          a hole that is from joining,
& to which we hasten
                 over the deserts of the hand, to breathe.

THE EMPRESS

boar in the dark thicket
spotted with sun

                    it is
something I have never seen

come out to play
at the feet of his friend

lying down beside her
for no rest

                but being thus
an animal near the mother
or matrix of animal
                    form

that lady with her own
problems
                by the brim of a
small cool fountain

                    the sound
of which has
nothing to do
                with her music

except that it never stops

WRONG CIRCUMSTANCE

The gods had come,
Zeus led them
steel-cuirassed,
a conquistador

up Whaleback ridge
& all dawn long
they said their meanings
under the pines;

all that while I
followed her I thought
was Love & who knew me
as if she knew no other

& led me dark ways
weary inside her
till she let me go—
I met them coming down,

finished with their
music, & in that company
Love was walking
in her own place.

REACHING THE LIMITS

Dust flats, the hills are competent
          to grease this land down
          & make it fat, a swelling
out of the city, non-human reek elaborate
in the shunned air. Driving out in brick heat
          where scattered trees explain
          the structures of Pindar
turned outward from the common measure, a tower
but a tower only of light. We see.
If the soul does not see, no wind blows rains fall
& the steps go up, into the sunlight, banished in the bright eye

We see the mortal brightness of the sun crackling
through the young willows. We see. Perishing eyes,
perishing lungs, perishing hands. I thought I told you not to touch me.
Be grateful I have hands. Or touch me. Do you know
how it is to be touched this way, killed by a bird cry
coming too soon? The soul, seeing into you. Make them stop.

All day the soul sings for a breath of air, prances to breezes,
vomits its quick learning in the caressing shade.
          The problems
          of Pindar's melody
          or to grasp
          a complex order
    outside the easy music of the head. Or let it touch me.

MUNGO'S PERPLEXITY

for Roi

Africa & where I
find love is
highlands, Africa
where the animals
meet, the tyger
& the hippocamp
if we are waiting
together in the shade,
love sweet sick
ormolu Africa,
green fern lace
bridesmaid of the
Muslim East,
black Africans
with full mouths
smiling & kings
of highlands, ac-
tually eating
food o let me
drape my imagined
kingdom on your
sweaty necks
& know Africa
as first home
of what we do
to get like this
after it all
is said & said
again, I will
give up Wordsworth
if you promise
to make everything
new around us &
not to kill me,
we will get married
only when you are at
the brink of childbed

where gets born
the great monster
of the agony
of your every day
who will leave
me alone & will have
nothing to eat.

THE ROAD AT THE EDGE OF THE DRAW

To J.R.

to hold night
up to the light

& see it move
black figures

against the cup,
earth, voyage,

closing the doors
of my house

I wanted
to walk in woods,

be alone
against the sky,

my own
outline thick

against
the drift

of my beginnings,
give all

over to trees
pine needle

strew, confuse
the path.

O rich opinion
of her body,

measure of such
ends &

purposes as mine,
the art

is not enough
I ask for.

The light
stands by itself

or seems to,
blue soaked

out of the sky,
a wind moves

about the trees.
The wall's a

walk, each limit
a destination,

the loneliness
is to stand

alone or pressed
together,

one principle
to make

& make it over,
a naked word

among the music,
one body

& forget
my shaping

of it
as you

hands folded
out of sleep

pray
a god you

only dream of
whose name

is ice or
fire, long

night with
no beginning.

It is not
the name

that you remember
but silence

that lives in
that same world

or maybe music
when the dance

has moved off
to another

& still
hear it,

see
bodies moving

inside the trees,
white legs in leaves

or one body
walking

a little
before me

arms
at her sides

remote
from my

conclusions,
legs

brushing the
leaves back,

closing
the circle.

V

Vulva, do you know it now?
To find the cunts of things,

                                        to come in. God spare us the chill
of old bones. To go in. O my god the glory of her touch
her body moving

                        When you know this,
right past the story, right into the true time.
Cunt is now. Caught in its folds we grow wise.
Volaspo, words of the Volva, wisewoman, woman part that knows
all.

    This is the future. This is now.
When it all comes.
                        The story
                                I told you
is the night, of lovers burned into blue stars, comes.
To come is to come true.

                        That is now, finding it at last & going in.
It is the hour when the dance stands still, noon or midnight,
at the place of perfect fit.
                        The instruments,
of giving & taking,
                making & hearing,
                                are perfect.

                        The shaping
of our concerns
                by what they draw close to
when the bird
                settling to the ground
becomes its shadow

                the story & the world come true

                                        (from *At the foot of the letter*)

THE STAR MAP

the way to look
for them in
darkness
to set shapes
upon what we
do not see
that do not
show them
& this im-
position
resolving
an uncertain
number
of variable
lights
into the outlines
of a picture
we are taught
to think we
see
    is using
the map & the
drag of Babylon
Egypt & those
desert places
where rising
Venus as
evening star
projects
such light
as makes
real shadows
of real women
on that

flat ground
             that
single clarity
drags us
year after year
to such inspec-
tions star maps
urge us
             to see
some stars a fish
or ten a winged
horse for the
sake of gills
in the wet air
horsefeathers
                 or
for the sake
of the woman
the light struggles
to disclose.

ATTENTIONS

for Paul Blackburn

(inland seagull cry
(of a bird
(red ink cannot draw

Paul the birds that hunt
rough throated
call us to swift care

whose instruments they
are & find
bearing by their food

as they pluck soft
exactness
from the shells of words

    Or, accuracy is what you can eat,

        care that property whereby you find your house

        a method of holding your way &
        sending your voice down to hunt

& *method* going
           along a road

                a motion
to accord with the stretch of road

                    by the lay of the land to know

what if anything lives there.

THE GYMNASTS

Lords of the burnt glass, the bullwhip wielders,
dark in their dreams of standing in-between,
the dancers, lords of the dance, who make the foot
fall & rise in the living circle, the night where
blood is a fire, lords of that night, elaborate,
urgent, who make the dancer fall, break her bones,
twist her sinews so she walks the circle, lords of instrument.

The amulet maker, secure in his dark bazaar,
vaunts his wares, boasts you will celebrate such sex,
walk invisible with them, dance, break out of the circle.
Believe him & lose the measure of each act. Hold song,
hold the upswelling of live flesh, sing in all your body.
Your flesh a talisman, listen to me you who are weary of
games at no stake, coveters of air.

It is not accomplishment we care for, none but the feel
of their bodies, their opening nakedness, the ritual of a solid
unyielding body mastering light & air. Keep
touch, be of the dance, this music.

(A FAMILY HISTORY)

after the letters
                'My love, you will ride
in a carriage'
                with all the fine ladies,
Karachi, 1865
                & nothing else left
of the failure of that love
or its success
                beyond the wildest
gold Indian dreams of even Samuel,
                from whom, perhaps,
into her hands
                greatuncle John some
gold pieces & that was that.

(for Timotha)

The room & the floor & the opening door
because it is part of the air

                      in early morning
careful of your hands, unlock the light
coming from Africa & give yourself pleasure
in your unsolved self, who is beautiful
& lives
        all the years you have not yet
convinced yourself to be
                  while all the while you wear
their skin on your skin, their flesh on your bones

That this room is key to a bigger room
the light sucks in & out of
                  a sea beach
of light regarding you & holds you holds you
when you move
              eastward from your evening
when you think it is dark when you think
yourself alone when you think there is no one knows you

CLIMBING ALL THE WAY UP THE BODY

                                        the feet are spirit
the hands tomorrow, the throat in the fire
as the earth itself sings

                        November & dead fields.

Cosmology is perception.

                    The arch
                                meeting & parting
                        of legs
            supporting, & moving what they hold—

                                that matter
is vector, mass a motion
                teaches us what moves is movement, as my
body is,
                orient. my sun goes up. moves.

                        & flesh's Kind is a kind
of motion.
            Time, too easy, how we make
                        our moves. What

are you going to do.
                Now. Or about.
                            This.

                        All round it
turning & the moon falls
                cosmos is percept
                                moves.

VESALIUS

the man who knew the design
of our bodies
    that our Mean
or due proportion of spirit
is how much necessary flesh,
to spell it

   here,
run your fingers on it
musculature of delight
that moves for you
& always towards you

        it is said
to be behaviour of animal
tissue
  & never mind
but it is the field
     & there are
bees between it & the next
moving among them
      even
in due measure though you
cannot see them you can
hear them always

    Think
about the bees & then
forget them
   who are the
movements of your movements

And I have walked across the sea
on the waves that are dolphins that are poetry
from Ionia, king or captive

deiknumi, I point out,
                              across, or in the pattern
of the woven cloth
                  recurrences,
                              or where I come again
to the same place
                  & it is not. That is as simple as
a flower or better
a story

          told as I saw it, *oraō*, I see
a man take a sword & jab it deep
in the wall of his house
                              & light bleeds through the cleft
so it is day
                  Not having come
                              Being there
where the city is,
                  all time.

          & being from Ionia, Yawonia,
have little need of women
                              except when the Great Lake wind
detains me,
                  filling with grey reek ·
the proximate city.
                              In the cloth I carry
or carries what I am,
                              bleached the sail cloth
bleached the fierce sea.

LIVONIA AVENUE

            not to center
            though I live too
            nearby

                    Livonia to where the tracks end
                    curve to the sheds south &

            the double back

                                    lots

                                            spread

    in midwinter space

                    New
    Lots to take its name,
                            urgent of no
    faint promise or godlike yield

    streets radial
                    to no center
                    or with respect to none

                        •

(the printer)

    job-sad steely Baltic mind
    conjoint with pride of craft
    & goof-off self-sad cunning,

    this was the gunning of him
    over such endless avenues in slush
    to get to whom
                        urgencies of **a dozen's work** of
    verses in my arms & somewhat
    mad elevations of within my hat

                & never paid him
    for lack of a clear bill

nor would he ever render one
stubborn as I am, he in his own mind
              (or so in unrewarded
labor of whose hands & offset eye
a magazine of verse begins)

                    •

under el arches
stone courses carrying
trains over Linden
a shout a horn roar
seizes the air
                    grinds
the concrete walls down
faster
        the words cut in them
whom Connie loves
& what she does with him,
her number being

chiseled in the wall's roughcast
combed down with what makes
concrete smooth or her lips red

the pebbles
                    white or
schyst so gleaming
                    (opaque or
trans-
        lucent, a name
upright in a dream)
                    caught

                    •

the greeneyed girl
of someone's
bad dream

hugged the girder
on the platform
pressed

to its iron angle
turn & turn
about

now this time
her back crushed
to it

her green eyes fixed
along the diminishing
tracks lead

out into Brooklyn
& from it back
lightless again

●

wild lots where women
were only in dream re-
garded :
            whose flesh in
actual practice no one
wanted,
          the burden of it,

thrice-greatest Hermes
is Venus,
            Hermaphrodite
palpable beneath her skirt

not deep down
her well the thrust
he'd give
but her face
a look
an agony of smug a-
bandon leering
in her eyes,
              his eyes
discovered such small
joinings

       no matter
as long as green
& evil luring mindless
sexual were her
eyes

who stopped in arch or station
glued by his longing to that
abstract cunt of a night-time
woman
       left dangling in his own

uneasy dark, far off red eyes
of the train at last & at last
bearing down

          •

      I too got
      into that story
             late one night
in cold
      from where such
trains turned out their lights I walked
two miles in the dense clear still cold

great squares, russian avenues of another time,
intersections of blind streets with here & now
where I shuddered at the side-wind from the alleys
turning me round to find
              after a few blocks
a pack of wild dogs walking with me
silently
close at my heels
         fanned out behind me
         & little by little around me
till I walked among
half a hundred animals
            I would not count them
stepping with never a sound be-
side me all the way home.

face at the shadowed door
torque of her body away

I walked ten blocks further
wondering what I saw

RUNNING EYES

a svaha for Richard Clarke

Dakota
I didnt see it.

Vermont
a month.

A life
in this place—

new lambs
for old,

we are crucified.
Massachusetts.

———————————

Signing my name with a chisel
I hear the blackbird
trapped in the stone

        let
        let me
        let me
        out
of your stupid doctrine

———————————

The printers found
one page could
not be bound.

"was a en she
accompa uncle
goat, me erself
leading gnus,

r hair laugh
Her eye Inca
double iverin
made he sun

love, ad of a
where arvel at
eading e birds
me now? ok in"

They said the author's
Orpheus
& tore him to bits.

She-printers,

invention of poetry.

———————————

walking by the Delaware
I believe it all again

Remembering the Delaware
I believe it all again again.

———————————

Three days on three months
my head breaking with the question
What is man's soul, does each
have one, how
can it thrive,

I saw a cloud
shaped like a cloud. In the

sky it was.

Trouble with country houses
mouse-shit.

       That bolt
of yellow silk I bought
so long ago in Sinkiang,
those falling leaves.

               Mouse-shit everywhere.

Church wedding, swelling organ.
Church funerals, passing by.
               Secular means forever.

Frog on lily pad:
Do what thou
wilt shall be the whole
Splash

Once upon a time
forget this story

Once there was an
end to the whole thing

Once there
never mind

Long ago & far

A way.

Up the narrow road the broadbacked bull
carried the old man : Lao-tse

is fleeing his native land,
disgusted with adjectives.

The worst of it all
is private death.

Amanita muscaria,
or deadly sight.

Running on my eyes
I am clumsy with my hands.

These things
I think
I see.

SALT STORY

(for G: & S:)

Their lives are quiet.

Bent over the crucible
he dreads the coming of the red-bearded one
who turns everything to food
& the food to shit.

He sends out for pizza
gets caught.
He goes to jail.

Coming back years later in his shiny new parolee's suit
he digs down deep under the sumac
to retrieve that buried equation
cached there before they got him.

As it solves itself in his hands,
the equinox!

a knock at the door

a tree full of red beards.

THE OBSEQUIES

a disease long in his atmosphere
caught him doing another man's work

hunks of bread glasses of coffee a window
high over the empty street
that was how it got him, he didn't
love anybody any more
& maybe worse

    I woke up knowing I could shift
my death onto another if I acted fast

but all the needles of his life
pointed in the same direction, the clock
by which he lived slipt into 4th & ran,
in a dark corner quill-pens floated quietly
out of his reach

    he opened a certain oracular book
found the sea was inside it, fell into the sea

If I could tell you but I keep my secrets

                              it is a shape I am trying to discover
                              like the raised arms of the woman
                              reaches out of the mountain of the west
                              to take the sun in, two arms raised

like an open mouth.

                    I will repeat things over & over again
because in the spaces between repetitions the undiscovered shape will take form,

as we have always talked in the interstices, not at the intersections, of a
web of discourse. Talk.

                    I am willing to concede that accidents happen:
in Kenneth Anger's book on Hollywood
an unnamed cocksucker
                         describes blowing Rudy Valentino as
"Direst communion with the divine."

                         I have no way of knowing if he meant
"direct"

        & am waiting for accidents to happen. Or the naked woman, side
of a dire road, agonist of a drama occurs only in my mind but that she
is lost from the inner theater into a tangible world.

                              Is lost into matter
& becomes a shape. Or the road itself tonight wetslick under haze under moon.
Light on in an empty house.

Forget all things   •   which god
invoke first touching the stove   •   cooking
            morning coffee, sun
off stones outside, deep-limed, rough wall
            taking the sun in

                     Forgot
where the sugar was   •   kicked into
the standing empties, scattered, spin
            the bottle   •   point
where my heart points   •   which sun or shade
            receives this day's homage,
which god. Forgot
                her warm sleeping body
stretched half uncovered   •   Somewhere,

between the sugar & the milk, he forgot
            why he was there or who
she was or what a woman was or why
            restless suns
moved across the sky   •   Where does my
            heart point he thought

& wanted a ritual of morning   •   Deny the night
his hands thought, lit that first
            cigarette of freedom
the dizzy-maker, soma god on altar, howled
in his quiet thought. This is new day   •   summer
            heat beneath the bottom of the pot
where the flame had been   •   ritual   •   rough wall
            took the Sun in.
            takes sun in.

SONATA

Three doors & through each a woman.

The first waited in her flesh   the other
walked right in   a ring
on her little finger   the third sang
something through the door

                    A dead man
in a locked room
with three open doors. Two open doors.
An open
door.

        Beyond the city of Purgatory
the discontinuous soul waits for the County bus.

        It is nowhere near on time, & raining.
        In his hand a piece of paper:

He who had been inside is outside. Take the first form again.

Before midnight
before the mass
I wouldn't worship
I walked

in the old
neighborhood
& the tough bone
of a blonde face

took my eye & held
it even with her
body tight in the
thin pink dress

we passed but she
called out
she had a kid
with her

said Why do your
eyes look that
way I mean I've
always known them

o jesus you
used to live here
that's why,
it doesn't count

that explains
why you look
that way it
doesn't count

But I could see
her left breast
loose of the low
stencilled dress

went with her &
said well the first
thing to do is
get you rid of the kid

& out of the old neighborhood.

A QUINCUNX

Welcome symbol needs of early morning after too much nada
all the night: I dreamed we were brothers or sisters
we remembered the house in Kansas where we were born
I dont know where you are I smell you there were the same
number of elm trees in the yard I see you I smell your breath.

HELIXES

Grey as a squirrel

                    the squirrel

tunnels in sunflower seed,

                              a day so wet the husks

cling to his brush of tail

                         matted light, an almost

invisible rain

               His feet

move easily on the wet seeds

                              whether

he finds what he's

                    looking for or not

he still keeps eating

                    These are years

we burrow in

                    our time of need & to

do it & be alone in the rain

                         I love you

always more & never

                    the same as easy

as it is to say it

                    we keep going & it is not

easy

            "living the other's death, dying

the other's life"

                    if I increase

you are diminished

                        & only when they are

at opposite ends of the sky

                            does the moon

take the sun's

                full brightness

a certain

            knowledge no place could

be so close

            no flesh could be so one

again

        & if you rise I fall

                        There is no

logic to it but to cling

                        to the uttermost

in ourselves, the uttermost

                in each other

& not be less

         than the furthest reaches

hunger anger

       or even

love would let us be.

            Each

morning is a window

            & through it we can see

the shadows we throw

             through the cold glass

do not trouble him

           where his problems drive him

or where

        hidden in the husks of our world

he looks for them

         to suck that secret

makes these shells flowers

            & the flowers turn

day after day

        to one same sun.

A FABLE

                    once was a woman
showed her
self
all through the psyche
of the town,
her hairy
lipped sisters
particularized
Eros:
        'watch
out for serpent
Love
        dont waste your
time you
hear me on
him'

        so the woman
long past
her girlhood
looked in the night
on naked Love

who stirred in the
light, said
'wont you ever
let my trust
go on sleeping
in the dark
of our mutual
intentions,
turn off the light
& dont look at me
with the eyes of the
town in your eyes'

so she went
back & told her
sisters 'it
happened just
like you wanted
he looked at me
& saw you
looked at me
& saw for the
first time
the whole
stinking family
the whole
town what
will I do
now I am
vanished
into everything
else'

& they laughed
& brought out wine
in slender
corinthian jars
& they said

'it will not
make any
diffference
after a while

if a man
really loves
a woman
he will take
the sour
with the sweet
& will respect
her connections
& the society

from which she rose'
& they drank
wine & gave some
to Psyche

who went home
drunk & said to
Eros "I am
not a woman
I am your Wife
use me
after the intricate
customs of your
secrecy

& let me shine
in the darkness
of what you are"

but Eros said
'we have lived
here too long
even the rocks
are the town's
rocks & the trees
drink poison
from the shadows
of the townfolk
on their roots
we must build
a labyrinth
to hide the monster
of our perfected
love'

& Love
hid themselves
in his city.

Loves that wield their english in us

pricking on the great plain
                          table of the game
where nothing is
                  but what insists itself
into movement
morning grey specific dove
                          humming at her feet, in her
shadows
            she is breaking branches
at the rim of the wood   She is walking
in loose clothes

            My *she* & my *loves* are simple
deceitful but not vague
sun in new grass darkening lightening

the blur is in the eye too close
but her lips at the rim of the world
taste precisions,
                  all our empty elm trees
all our precisions.

GENERATIONS OF THE MEN

(for G:L:)

& the work to be done
(I am not so scared I will eat history
nor death on my specific back
                              bharami
I do carry
            not)   Grasses grow through rocks.

This is our root
stock:
            growing surrounds time
connects all points of the circle
in a straight line
                        which is the stalk
up. You looked for leaf where there had been flower
Earlier.
            We drank that tea already.

(i.e., Halsey & Gates
run parallel
through Brooklyn
join
in the first pastor
of Gates Mills, Ohio
                        where the river carries the bridge across)

There was loneliness. There was wisdom. There was a green
stream under trees I dont know.
                              The fire in your hearth
is a sea.
            Boats in Sahara. Haroun's electric battery.

Now the girls of Ohio were wearing short skirts.
                              There is work to be done.

Never until the god-saturated streets reach the heart
& the road to Cleveland never starts.

Christ was a kind of bridge but there wasno river.
It is what we made: *and then Elpenor came*
reeking of private destinies.

                    I came here because I was afraid.
Black tunnel through which I passed
to a beautiful mouth I used to know & kissed his lips.
Brownhaired who did not believe, what a
sweet mouth
                or dream. A white church,
a burden of time to bear over the water. And not mistake.

The trees I didn't know. White-faced calves. The mothers
the woods full of mothers.
                      Devil I worship them
in flesh which is not cow
                      or is the crinkle of dry ground
weight of our feet in mud
                    you looking for coltsfoot,
the pressures, to shape the world.

Elpenor. I Ulysses too have slept in Circe's window.
Trees following the stream. I thought of our friend as Leda
mastered, holding the world by his cunt. Not to let go.
Not to fall.
              Work to be done. New masteries.

Our star Uranus the false malefic
l'énergie psychique indifférenciée, the libido
itself.
        Hold on & be nice to people
kat' ergon, according to the work.
To be done.
              The work to be done is not to be done.
No masteries. He did not believe
in anything he could touch. If it was he. If I dreamed.
History is documented fantasy. Homer said
Tell me, muse or *Sing to me*.
Fat Virgil said *I sing*.

Homer knew no history. He knew Event.
No filiations. Filiations.

Because our fathers
tease strangers, flyte with the new-entered guest,
mock on the bridge between persons,
                              make up the
mysteries & defile the mysteries, because they like
to look at naked magazines
                         we are brought forth
into the valley. This lily filiation
onto the dungheap
                 where mangled by pig (by cock by snake)
becomes our rose.
                 There was a kitchen door
& the wind blew through it. There was dust on the road.
A truck passed.
                 The generations of men
sing & demand their song. Work to be done.
Girls to be stripped of clothes. Hell
of its inadvertencies. Words of their ease.
He followed the stream
came to the source
a great isolate
swan swam thereon.
                 Canada geese
on your pond
year after year.
                 Binding themselves, an obligation
to their medium. The comeback.
Song of the wind in the kitchen door.
The dogs
belling
deep in the inner structure of the house.

In the valley of the Chagrin,
closer to time.
                 White church kiss ease
                 time water trees. Force
of the original mechanism.

                    aeide thea
Geauga County. The radiant earth. The work.

VAJRAS

1

Come through the water
come through

                                  Red light

                    stone
                    from
                    which
        a bird of thunder flies up
                              off
  to the places of
               fierce going
      goes.

2

my frien' he
wanned to
talkto
navaho

he said
hello

      the empty valley said
navaho ochre
          navaho gold

3

this is *ta'wil*
            rootwork

         the leading back
               (explicare,
            elicit the tree
                    from its branches)
using the root

PRONUNCIATIONS OF AN UNVOWELLED TEXT

(to the memory of Jack Spicer)

Light & the secret
message all sides,

Out west they hark
at Capt Midnight
: old crow
              (from bleeding
frontier, the) boxtop
decoder.
           Mr Ree
(not Kansas, Ken,
Tuck) Mr Ree I
kidlike
(played: a game)

                        he
(on a board, little
lead gun, little lead
phial wherein
caput mortuum,
sludge of words:
his death by
poison)
           he, Ree,
wanted to know
(rooms of the house
lilac & gold,
library bedroom
gazebo parlor)
what room of the
house what
got done in.

           Guess.

What room
would you.
                Light
all sides
will, seek red
holy books.
                I
understood this
flame, & didn't
burn.   O.K.

First theme.

(2)

The second thing I wanted to say
was this. There. Was a pain.
It was real. We fell out
of the discourse.
                    Tomorrow
never knows they say. That's
a secret. A secret chanting
into itself.
                At. Times. One
has to sing into one's glass,
one's empty glass. Two's a
threesome. The second
I wanted to say a thing was this:

there is a pain, it is Hawthorne's
black veil over Jack's face,
black face over my face,
black mouth for our. No.

Know. Our meat. Every
man jack. It is black.
A black
        looking
          seven
      glass years ba
dluck.

Lofted by which wind
the compass smashed
on the brittle sea.
                    Men
with beards are hiding
something: Human faces.

The second I wanted a thing
was to say this, hide your
stupid comprehending faces,
dont be so fucking understanding,
so few
secrets left.

(3)

But (largo) it's all a.
That's what I read
in the unpapers, all up &
down the breadth of the
land (postcard from
Tombstone) the badged
dragomans of the Law
spin
        their tin decoders.
That was the secret
script,
            in & out.
                        Wall
scratch & jakes scribble:
textus receptus
(your god is an ass),
Indus valley ringaleavio,
hide &.   Christ,
you secret savior, tongue
(divine) in (human)
cheek. Knew
all the logical
manipulations.
Soft palms of his hands.
So few?

Every face a
crater blasted
by unrecorded cosmic
Shook. Black veil.
What matter. Does.
Our flesh its code,
nothing but secrets.

House
to hide lares in.
The wise man
hides his god.

(4)

Stressed
(stretto
too)—the
house dick
is—after
all—your
friend,
        guest's
friend a private
law,
    we can square
him
    (even this grass),
the house dick's
our secrets,
logbook
of the restless hotel

(5)

"it will
take a lot
of new ideas
to reveal
its secrets"
                    (ad for the ocean)

this house
who lived?
a secret
voice
under the door

was the sea

(feared
ghost by keyhole—

what room did what
fall out
in?

a plain text
escorting
some widowed
intention,

text no
plainer than
song)

(6)

Not hide more meaning.
o Marsyas sang a
secret song,
      (Apollo left
holding the
slough of it)
      who knew
ben trobar
& find what
hid in the wood
he whistled
(may have been words),
clus
  where music other
than in among?

Withwit.
Elfsprawl athwart,
newspaper
from Hyperspace
              building who through—
the word cube
springs open,

Jack in the
              by be bo bu ba box—

(7)

ghost holes
overtone
from anguish of
(in death the)
phoneme,
echoic
        (ghost)

trace of a
————truth————

        true   false
        true   false
        true   false
        true

                              he pulled the zipper
                              the bird
                              flew

(the bird falls)

                        (Code)

no more secret than
a woman somebody

else loves &
we dont, do we,

ever after, understand
but try to. He did

& opened the window.
Opened the street.

What did you there?
Watched

men travel from different places,
added apples & pears.

(To a girl named Nancy)

You were sixteen &
knew who I was too

It did not matter
as long as the style
was there & it was
sweet.
      New.
            No matter
that our bodies
betrayed each other's
(sense of)
          beauty—

this is called
living in the world.
God
      would call it
eating shit.
          You
loved my voice
& in my dreams I see
the clean
adjectives of your jaw.

pain
if animals only
or only the
animal part

felt
it or bore,

but I know the shape of the black pines
stand against the sky given the slightest moon

I know the experiments of those blossoms, those so-
called lotuses inside us as they struggle

towards a light
that is outside
they must

with root force
breaking rock

tear through us to
flower in

SONG IN THE CRACKS OF LIPS

around these darkness

let a will be weft

& be shuttle fond upon itself

for all the celebrations of the Hidden Face

ΦΒΚ

warming   warming
two suns were not enough

Her footstep sealed in water,
gypsy fish nibbling

as if by the dirt in my fingernails
know my thought on all these matters

an understanding of a process,

by which the images are stretched

taut, trued

to the perceived, so strung

as to give sound,
                   hold the note & allow

the mind to handle it

tone upon undertone.

the marshes we
continue

too wet
to plant

she pulled herself together
acre by acre

dry land & wet
wet land & too

wet to plant in

where everything grows by itself and

it was where I lost
& found you last night,
my morning crumpled
mouth knew nothing of it,

the one sea-gull
above our house
spoke it, spoke
from the middle of his slow

wheeling, creaming
the tahini
white with water
I remembered,

the spoon's round
understanding
remembered
you beneath me.

MOEURS ETERNELLES

I am 31 years old & last night's coffee
sweet good & cold

does not begin
to fill up my mind—

I made love late & dreamt of alchemists
there are many colored pens

& a prism on the table
bad music on the radio

& in the pot where five chrysanthemums wither
new sprouts arise

it would be easy to mistake this place

UNDER THE STAR GIEDI

(three for Gael)

"I wonder if she knew what I was saying?"
Plums. Butter on the table, somebody's child
crawling under it, & trees outside.
They grow up before you know it,
overnight a tree of heaven or a wild
young son eating his mother's heart.

She wanted to crawl between us & be warm.

————————————

Earth passage, sonnet in the night
"she's so screwed up"   any
repetition is a , sonnet, form, fix
in the tunnel,
                        "it's not grass,
it's not acid"   it's the vein
we travel down
                        chosen or rejected by each cell.

————————————

Hymnody of evening. I loved
your honesty, the plain
face you were beautiful in
& your nakedness I would always fall for.
You meant it. You
fell for it too, were wise

as only a victim can be wise.

FROM THE GOLDEN VERSES OF THE PYTHAGOREANS

Begin no work
before praise
to the Great Gods
                        (who were other
to our counsels,
I hear their music, 45s & cheap LPs
thin in the bass,
their bodies appear in the music
rarely, glint of prismatic light
off the turning vinyl,
hipbone shoved into view.
With my own eyes I have seen
a woman with too much money,
a pale snow-leopard
panting in the New York heat)
but the "archeologist
should have some training in anatomy"
tell how many were buried in one tomb's
pile of bones,
female or male,
how many gods buried in this
girl dreamy under the turning disc

& the Immortal Gods
who turned the moon on their anvil,
returned me to this place,
a secret song,
rain across the Greenpoint Park
stippling the sandbox,
so young a woman in her mauve rain-spotted dress
taut over sacrum, the song,
we rear instruction,
rain down Nassau,
who set this conjunction above me
moon into sun into dark.
Breaking the holy cross

Christ stretched on the zodiac.

& to the Demons of earth, the earth
conspicuous praise,
mustard on my shirt, turmeric
on Ganapati, sound of a horn,
celestial longitudes
(who can blow a horn these days
cool or sudden swung on the air
but the demons of the atmosphere
live in the sound, live in the curved
exponent of metal space,
face, demons have faces,
wind in the trees,
moon a horn we blow with our last breath)

temenos on hill, cairn,
upright song's
stone
touch & it sings
(the diamond also
rides on the grooves,
hisses, sings)
no girl outside—

ship tombs, burning boats over Kattegat.
Return, return.
Palimpsest of tissue, mind over mind,
cells return us to our turn,
sun spin, Carbonek,
wind in the trees.

And to the beloved
from whom no distance
kindly divides,
who finds in the brass
tacks of our winter culture
the green of copper & Mount Victory—
"on Puy de Dome
a man of brass
fifty cubits high
& called him Mercury,"

the beloved, to whom the demons of fire
whisper a ritual of water
for no worshipper but me
whoever I am,
& for whom the demons of air
initiate hot afternoons
& taste our sweat together,
the cave!   the cave
behind fire!

someone immensely naked:
it is that, tree,
I summon from your shade

when love's enemy is sleep
& dream love's siegecraft

opening the gates • love,
a confluence of people

on the one silver road,
pathways of order,
                    the company:

must make, must be
beyond what we are trained to take

as beauty,
beauty being the quality

or immensity of her undress
& we can talk to each other

when what we are doing is the milky way
travelling hand to mouth forever with our beautiful eyes

Caress the lips of natural order
impudent child at the Venus's foot

feeling the marble buttocks,
press as hard as you can

against the cleft & the form
stands firm.
           Break

all the leaves & all the trees
the cool thigh will still

brush your shoulder as you edge away.
You will grow old

beneath her unsmiling smile

(for Fontaine)

wait the roof of pale storms
May lightning up the southern face
over the sense of the city,

                           cool wind at dawn
green clouds on seabord

a women comes downstairs to start her car.
No birth is easy   •   Your house & my house,
seagulls stand on rooftree before the sun.

A woman comes downstairs to start her car,
her footsteps light with her body, her body
heavy with music she's been hearing
heavy with song   •   What song   •

starting the car   •   no birth is easy   •
no day for all our matter lucidly begins

IMAGES FROM THE PROCESS OF THE UNENDING WORK

(for Harvey & Timotha)

1

The sparrowhawks were there & a silver cup.
He wrote it all down, forming the word slowly

& fitting his memory of her body into the clay.
When the name was on it it breathed,

wondered why had it been so slow in coming,
loved him   •
    Sunlight

off the cup burnt his story away.
The birds settled down to the unassembled meat.

2

Sun energy baking her head   •
waking the dead   •
     having
    words & using them she
        ate everybody's supper
took her clothes off in the closet,
conquered the good humor of the air
       burnt brown.
I wanted to say a simple thing it   •   is

the face on the other

　　side of the voice

　　　　the way you

occupy my mind

　　my whole time

　　　　a tree

lives chaster off its roots than I

waiting

　　for a word to drop

　　　　like of course an

apple

　　from your lips

　　　　too far gone to eat

we rot

　　apart from each

　　　　other we do not

increase

　　if there is a leaf

it is there

on the branch

on the other

side of your anger

my angry

hands will not reach

but tear

what little we do

have away.

(at the last, for Gerrit)

the sumac
now black
almost
after rain
made tea
of the red,

maleate!
color of apples
& bitter
till the honey
(drink cold

astringent,
a quality
of an actual
world
a big red
glass of tea

I remember
in your much
frequented kitchen
sea birds
lighthouse
red tea with the

hairs of sumac
escaped the sieve,
the undivided
air over the
breakwater
holding the boat

Dahin,
dahin the old
initiate wrote
of such experience,
arms of the land
where the sumac
was red at Brace's
cove & the leaves
turned red
& the boat

went its way
where there was
nothing to say
but the sea.

THE TOWER

three islands
in the sea
(she & her & me
three islands
in the sea
Atlantic himself
out there
over the edge
(the land
we've just
these few
million years
come in from the
wet
we'll be back
dolphins
be back

three islands
off the coast of Maine
I am a man
I am a woman
I came here to find bread
make bread
(bake bread

bake bread
for Kali Yuga
("credit,
not money"
for Kali Yuga
when the house
has glass walls
the tower

stands delectably up
everything can break
everything
built to fall
(I fall for you
day after day
fur around your
cunt the brightest
center of my eyes this
morning
third eye
for the fourth age
pale as you are
you're Kali
Kelly's shakti
white woman
with dark eyes

so the window
(the money
is all we've got
(the time
the house
under the mountain
"who hath time enough
hath none to lose"
face of a clock
standing there
two hundred years
to give me
that instruction
(took
the clouds
drift to sea
(may be four
islands
one darker
a shape
against the out
bending coast
(Poseidon weather

just
above freezing
everything
flows

Kali Yuga
credit
nobody bakes bread
(but the first
three ages
are man's
& this last
the age of woman
where her cunt
finally takes over
& we go
from there
& wind up
always here

(my cock
learn
tantra
of this yuga

(the cat
is brave
runs through the door
then stops to look
at where his feet
obedient
to his hunger
have taken him
past caution
out
where there might
be meat

down there
yellow house
green trim

grey house
with snow
sixteen
floors down
will I start
like Bruckner
counting leaves
to turn
everything to number
& number to music
the natural
world frozen
in human will
(more girls
no girls allowed
this male
tower
alone with its
sunrise
the world
is stone
(stone
grows

Kali Yuga
age of salt
skeletons locked
in yabyum
(embrace
beyond the flesh
we learn
to fuck bone

grey clouds over
us the white
over the sea
gone
to our home
brightness
(thin women
beautiful

in how they move
stripped
down to that
least
most
movement
dark
flesh inside you
the way you move

Against death this density
overlay of grasses,
lords, the richness of your fields

the women walking in them
not
the evening, not even the harvest

but in the middle of our time

world we know something of & go
to sleep taste of on our tongues